50
SIMPLE
THINGS
YOU
CAN DO TO
PAVE
THE EARTH

7·21·91
FOR TOM & CAROL,
IMAGINE, THIS FROM
A COLLEGE DROP-OUT!
LOVE,
Darryl

50 SIMPLE THINGS YOU CAN DO TO PAVE THE EARTH

Darryl Henriques

Ulysses Press

This book is dedicated to the many friends and relatives (too many to list according to the publisher) who kindly opened their homes to me and my family during the exhilarating ordeal of writing this book.

Special thanks to Mr. Philip Abrams for his work as comedy consultant and to agent number one for getting me out of the Pentagon and saving my soul.

And to my CODA study group, especially C.J.—I would have never finished the book if I'd come to the meetings!

Published by:
Ulysses Press
Sather Gate Station
Box 4000-H
Berkeley, CA 94704

Library of Congress Catalog Card Number 90-71325

ISBN: 0-915233-31-2

Printed in the U.S.A. by the George Banta Company

10 9 8 7 6 5 4 3 2 1

Cover Designer: Tim Carroll

Some of the profits from this book will be donated to environmental groups.

Printed on recycled paper

ACKNOWLEDGMENTS

I would like to thank everyone who didn't work with me but who nevertheless made this book possible, including:

- Former recording artist Richard Nixon —for becoming the first human being to recycle himself.

- Former President Ronald Reagan—for realizing that one redwood is enough.

- Financier Donald Trump—for proving that excess is not enough.

- President George Bush—for realizing that broccoli is worse than taxes.

- Vice President Dan Quayle—for being elected vice president and ending up in the wilderness.

- White House Chief of Staff John Sununu—for recognizing that the greenhouse effect is really a computer game.

- Secretary of State James Baker—for putting Kuwait on the endangered species list (just a few days too late).

- Former Secretary of the Interior James Watt—for revealing that saving the earth was absurd in light of God's promise to destroy it.

- Former Presidential Candidate Michael Dukakis—for getting no mileage from a full tank.

CONTENTS

EASIER DONE THAN SAID

FOR THOSE WHO HAVE BEEN "COMMITTED"

INTRODUCTION

In my role as Third Vice-President of the Committee to Pave the Earth, not a day goes by without a million phone calls from concerned citizens yearning to decorate their communities in asphalt and cement. I assure them that no matter how small their town might be, giant paving machines will eventually transform their home into a miniature Times Square.

Without this continued paving of America, tomorrow will never look like what it's supposed to. The development of the earth has already given rise to skateboards and mini-malls and is about to result in nature's greatest creation, "post-organic man."

Only post-organic man can transcend his biological past and create a paved new world, free from the whim of indifferent nature. For far too long, man has been held hostage to bodily needs. Now that he is becoming post-organic, man can find more reliable and expensive substitutes for things he has previously been able to obtain only from nature.

Post-organic man is putting the art in artificial. Air conditioning is eliminating the need for air, Perrier is far superiour to anything that ever came out of a tap and processed cheese spread represents a vital stage in the creation of 100 percent artificial food.

As we know from *Star Trek* and the space shuttle, Earth is simply a launching pad for post-organic man's exploration of the universe. While few of us can hope to become the Columbus of outer space, we can all help by increasing our consumption of space commodities such as Tang and space tomatoes. In this way our children's children will be able to bring the benefits of civilization to all alien life forms regardless of the number of their limbs, means of locomotion or method of reproduction.

Most of the "50 things" described in this book are designed to complete the paving of the earth so that we can continue on to colonize new planets. Of course, a few timid souls will complain about the vast sums necessary to fund this grand adventure. But remember, this money won't have to be repaid until all of us are long gone. There's no sense compromising the present for a future that may never even come.

In the "Simple Things for the Simple-Minded" section, you're introduced to obvious activities like growing algae in your washing machine for fun and profit and warming your house with body heat. After reading the "Easier Done Than Said" suggestions, you can amuse yourself finding and re-decorating your own private parking space and donning designer disposable diapers to save water for the canals of Mars. In "For Those Who Have Been 'Committed,'" the final section, you'll confront post-organic man's ultimate challenges—stalking the wild space goat and recycling your own life cycle.

Read on, then, and remember— life is too long a row to hoe, so always use a tractor. Or, as the ancient Romans said, "First a path, then a trail, next a road and finally a ten-lane interstate."

Darryl Henriques
Committee to Pave the Earth
Los Angeles, 1990

WHAT'S
GOING
DOWN,

DUDES

THE GREENHOUSE
VS. THE WHITEHOUSE

HOT HOUSE FRUITS

"As earth's atmosphere heats up, mangoes will soon be growing in Minnesota. Cold climate residents will no longer have to travel to the tropics. They'll already be in the tropics! The energy saved on flights to Hawaii and the Caribbean can be used to melt the polar ice caps. Then, at long last, Antarctica can be developed."

—Friends of the Future

BABY, IT'S COLD OUTSIDE

"There's a good reason why every human being on earth wears clothes. This planet is too damned cold. That's why for the past 10,000 years humans have been burning wood, coal and oil like there was no tomorrow. They are desperate for that near- naked Southern California lifestyle."

—Committee to Extend the Sunbelt to Montana

GASES FOR YOUR GREENHOUSE

• *Carbon dioxide* (CO_2). Exhale more than you breathe in. If that proves difficult, hyperventilate and run everywhere.

• *Chlorofluorocarbons* (CFCs). Look for them in spray cans and spray your way to a warmer and more tropical tomorrow.

• *Methane* (CH_4). Farmers call it "cattle gas." Cattle call it "farmer's gas." So eat lots of legumes.

• *Nitrous Oxide* (N_2O). To increase levels of this marvelous chemical, insist that your dentist give you laughing gas, even when he's working on other patients.

AIR TODAY, NONE TOMORROW

IT'S AN ILL WIND THAT BLOWS NO CASH
"The beautiful thing about air pollution is that people love it so much they'll die for it. It's no surprise that New York and Los Angeles, the two smoggiest cities in the U.S., are also the most expensive places to live. Smog fuels the real estate market in America."

—Smog and Your Money

A SMOG FOR SORE EYES
"When people move from polluted cities to areas with clean air, where visibility exceeds one block, they develop a condition known as *horizonitis*. If not treated immediately by reducing visibility, *horizonitis* can lead to terminal dizziness. As a result, cities are installing smog machines to prevent deadly outbreaks. At this writing, Congress is considering legislation to set mandatory visibility limits."

—No New Horizons Newsletter

FROM NUKES TO A NEW YOU
"As nuclear power plants continue to leak and melt down, increased radiation in the environment will speed up natural selection. It's only a matter of moments before humans mutate into smog-breathing creatures. These new life forms, *homo smogian,* will have no use for oxygen (and will actually be allergic to it). Oxygen will become a controlled substance. The Oxygen Police (aka, the Ox Squad) will be charged with confiscating and burning it."

—Future Facts

OZONE LOOPHOLES

HOLEY NECESSITY
"It is vitally important that we create more holes in the ozone so that the space shuttle can get into orbit. The reason NASA scrubs so many missions is that the few holes we have rarely appear over Cape Canaveral. If we had known about this ozone shield, we wouldn't have built the shuttle in the first place."

—*Space Trucker Magazine*

BROKEN SHIELD A BUST
"The ozone shield only protects us from pansy pollen and the radiation of ultra violets. That's why we need to replace it with Star Wars. Then we'll be safe from nuclear weapons as well. And we'll rescue the aerospace industry at the same time."

—**Friends of Star Wars**

ULTRAMORAL RADIATION
"Now that ultraviolet radiation threatens life on earth, the choice is clear. Get dressed or die. At long last, sinful sunworshippers will disappear from the earth."

—**Ultramoral Majority**

SHUN THE SUN
"There is nothing to worry about. People can easily evolve from a daytime schedule to working the graveyard shift. Instead of summer vacations people will estivate and spend July underground watching summer re-runs on TV."

—**Society for the Prevention of Sunlight**

DEW DROP ACID RAIN

ACID RAIN AND THE END OF HISTORY

"For thousands of years man and nature were at odds. Now with the development of acid rain, they are able to cooperate in the reconstruction of the earth. Man produces sulphur and nitrogen oxides by such activities as driving to the Dairy Queen. Nature does its part by transforming these emissions into acid rain or snow. (You know you've got acid snow if your snowman keeps eating the chunks of coal you use for his buttons.)"

—Sour Grape Group

ACID TREATMENT

"Acid rain purges unwanted and unsightly life forms from lakes and streams. It is also able to stop the forests in their tracks when they try to recapture vacant lots. Military analysts claim acid rain is our weapon of choice in the undeclared war with Canada over the issue of who are the real North Americans."

—AAA (Acidic Association of America)

ROME WASN'T MELTED IN A DAY

"Did you know that unlike a neutron bomb, acid rain has the ability to melt buildings! It's only a matter of time before it obliterates landmarks like the Eiffel Tower, the Statue of Liberty and the original Radio Shack so they can be replaced with Styrofoam replicas that will last forever."

—Styrofoam Art League

THE ACID TEST

"Because nature acts in such a willy-nilly way, all rainfall is not equally acidic. Test your local rain by bathing your Persian longhair cat in it. If the cat comes out of the tub looking like a Siamese, you're in good shape."

—LSD (Litmus Society of Detroit)

HAZARDOUS TO
YOUR WASTE LINE

SOON IT WON'T BE

"If we had enough imagination, there would be no such thing as hazardous waste. For thousands of years no one knew what to do with sawdust. Then someone put his mind to work and rescued sawdust from the waste-bin of history. People began spreading it on barroom floors and pressing it into particle board. It's only a matter of time before someone discovers a valuable use for the millions of tons of hazardous waste produced each year. So as a good investment we're recommending that you buy up as much of it as you can."

—*Junk Bond Weekly*

SIGN OF THE TIMES

"The only thing wrong with hazardous waste is the bad press it receives. Those 'nabobs of negativity' in the media will never recognize that our ability to produce hazardous waste is actually a measure of our success as a nation. Instead of bemoaning its existence, we should celebrate National Hazardous Waste Day and take some home to bury in our private landfills."

—**Home Dumps of America**

HAZARDOUS WASTE KEEPS US FIT

"Hazardous waste is a vital element in preserving our humanity. As man further dominates nature and natural hazards disappear from the environment, we must replace them with manmade hazards to preserve our normal level of stress and anxiety."

—*Stress For Health Quarterly*

UNNATURAL SELECTION

GOD, MAN AND ANIMALS

"In Genesis, God in his infinite wisdom gave man dominion over the animals. Therefore, the only rational reason to save a species is to be able to dominate it."

—Society to Keep Man Number One

MARTIANS, MAN AND ANIMALS

"It is of the utmost urgency that man become the only life form on the planet. Otherwise when extraterrestrials arrive they could sign treaties with enemy species, endangering our very existence."

—Extraterrestrial Friendship Committee

A VANISHING SPECIES IS
A USELESS SPECIES

"If we can't eat you, wear you, experiment on you or pet you, you've got no business being alive. It's nothing personal. You don't see the family farmer raising a ruckus about the fact that he's becoming extinct."

**—Interspecies Committee
to Publicize The Facts of Life**

LIFE AFTER MEDIA

"Wildlife is disappearing into public television studios where animals star in nature shows and work for peanuts."

—Creative Animal Agency

GROUNDWATER IS DIRTY BY DEFINITION

"GROUNDWATER POLLUTION" IS REDUNDANT

"Water from the ground is dirty, muddy and totally yucky. How can you pollute something that's already polluted?"

—Committee for Truth in Labeling

UNCOMMON MARKET WATER

"Thanks to the purifying effects of fallout from Chernobyl, European bottled water is now free of all microscopic life forms. Fortunately for image-conscious Americans, it also costs more than tap water. Drinking it in front of friends improves your self-image and allows you to experience foreign cultures in the safety of your own home or health club."

—Foreign Water Bottlers of America

WATER WATER EVERYWHERE

"Luckily, 97% of the world's water reserves are in the oceans. As our love of salt grows, seawater will taste better than tap water. Some marine biologists predict that when we start drinking seawater, we will evolve back into sea creatures."

—Seawater Bottlers of America

SUPER POLLUTION IS THE SUPER SOLUTION

"If enough chemicals get into our groundwater, we'll be standing on a liquid gold mine. Groundwater will become the universal liquid. We'll be able to dry-clean with it, run our cars on it and clean our ovens with it. With any luck water will be the rocket fuel of the future."

—Polluted Water Bottlers of America

GARBAGE MAKES US HUMAN

GARBAGE MAN
"Archaeologists teach us that man is the garbage-producing animal. If human beings stop producing garbage we could slide down the primate scale and find ourselves stuck somewhere between a ring-tailed lemur and a howler monkey."
—Landfill Association of America

THE GARBAGE OF EDEN
"Garbage scholars speculate that Adam and Eve left the Garden of Eden because there was no garbage pickup and the place became a dump."
—Bible Academy of Garbage Studies

LANDFILLS SAVE ENERGY
"By covering depressions in the landscape, landfills make the surface of the earth smoother. This enables the earth to move more easily through space, saving huge amounts of orbital energy."
—Smooth Earth Society

GARBAGE IS HISTORY
"Every landfill will provide clues to future archaeologists about the incredible lifestyles of the present day. These repositories of our hopes and dreams will be much more valuable than libraries because, unlike books, garbage never lies."
—U.S. Garbage Foundation

SIMPLE
THINGS
FOR THE

SIMPLE-
MINDED

1. KISS YOUR GRASS GOODBYE

Without lawns, croquet will become extinct.

BACKGROUND. More than anything else, the lawn represents America's love affair with nature. So it's no surprise that every year 27 trillion gallons of water are used to maintain this vital part of the eco-system (not to mention millions of pounds of pesticides to keep the grass looking the way nature intended).

TURF AND TURF
• Since there is not enough water in the world to provide a grass lawn for everyone, astroturf is the lawn of the future.

• Because it's not alive, it never needs mowing—just use a leaf blower to rid it of dirt and debris.

• During a drought you can paint it brown to show solidarity with neighbors whose grass lawns have died.

• **Astroturf Alert.** Unless your astroturf lawn is fenced off with a 20-foot high chainlink fence, professional football teams may at any time invade your yard and begin scrimmaging.

• **Astroturf Mega-Alert.** If an NFL team shows up and demands 500 million dollars to play league games on your astroturf lawn, it's probably the Los Angeles Raiders.

DID YOU KNOW?
• Rolling around naked on a "real" lawn can lead to severe itching or even dermatitis.

• From space, it's impossible to distinguish between grass and astroturf.

• In some parts of the country, sinkholes large enough to swallow cars can appear overnight in a natural lawn.

- Some scientists believe the lost city of Atlantis was actually swallowed up by a sinkhole in Orlando, Florida.
- Archaeologists from Disney World are currently excavating the site for a new attraction called "Atlantis Land."

DID YOU ALSO KNOW THIS?
- If all the water used on lawns in the U.S. was diverted to raising cattle, we could produce at least 10 billion more steaks per year.
- Would you rather mow the lawn or barbecue a steak?
- Once you eat a steak all you have to do is pick your teeth, but a lawn requires constant care.

THE LAWN GOODBYE
- With the water you've conserved by installing astroturf you can create terraced rice paddies in your backyard.
- Build a trendy new water park featuring giant wave machines, riptides and whirlpools.
- Flood the street in front of your house and transform it into valuable riverfront property.

THINGS TO DO
- Build a dome over your astroturf yard and use it year-round for lawn bowling, badminton and field hockey, not to mention quoits.
- Don't tell your neighbors that your lawn is astroturf and drive them insane with jealousy as they try to grow a lawn as beautiful as yours.

2. NO DIVING
IN THE CARPOOL

Carpooling is dangerous because conversations in cars can cause accidents.

BACKGROUND. The major problem with carpooling is that when one person wants to ditch work to go to the ballpark, everybody in the car has to go along. This costs industry 45 billion dollars a year in lost productivity, but does allow major-league baseball to schedule weekday doubleheaders.

CARPOOL TO OBLIVION
• Do not speak to the operator while the vehicle is in motion.

• They are easily distracted and forget where they are going.

• Workers from one company often end up at other companies.

• A few years ago fun house mirror fabricators were carpooled to the factory making the Hubble space telescope.

• The stealth bomber was designed by artists from the set of *Batman*.

SOLO DRIVE TIME
• For many Americans, the only time they get to spend alone is in their car.

• The automobile is the closest thing to a monastic retreat in America.

• Great spiritual quests are taking place as drivers meditate in their BMWs.

• That is why the principle of karma is named after the car.

JUST SAY NO TO CARPOOLING
• Give the carpool lane back to the solo driver.

• Replace all multipassenger vehicles with single-seat cars.

3. GONE WITH THE WATER

If it turns out that earth is the only planet in the universe with water, pray for rain! And don't be surprised when your water bill goes up.

BACKGROUND. Europeans use five percent as much water per capita as Americans. If we used water at the same rate as Europeans, we would have enough water for over five billion people. In plain language, that means if we save too much water, every human being on earth could move to the United States.

WASTING WATER FOR NATIONAL DEFENSE
• Wasting water may be the only way we can stop the rest of the world from moving here.

WASTING WATER FOR MENTAL HEALTH
• The reason everyone wants to move here is because, according to a recent government study, Americans are the most mentally healthy people alive. The reasons for this are as follows:

• A three-hour bubble bath has the same cure rate as ten years of psychoanalysis.

• A two-hour shower with pulsating shower head puts you in closer touch with your feelings than five years of primal scream therapy.

• A forty-five–minute sitz bath gives you a better self image than three years of gestalt therapy.

WASTE WATER TO SAVE WATER
• When you waste water, you create less water.

• When there is less water, there is less water to waste.

• And finally, when there is less water to waste, you end up saving water!

4. BODY HEAT
YOUR HOUSE

If the average temperature of the U.S. rose just six degrees, we could save 182 million barrels of oil a year—not enough to service our automobiles, but heck, we've got to start somewhere.

BACKGROUND. For decades, oil has been wasted by people using it to heat their homes rather than to run their cars. If people get cold, then they should get in their car, turn on the heater and drive somewhere. Staying home and burning oil won't get you anywhere.

BODY HEAT

• One of the cheapest and most efficient sources of heat is good old body heat.

• If your house is cold then it's obvious that there are not enough people in it.

• To heat a house with body heat the President's Council of Home Body Heaters suggests ten adults for every 200 square feet.

• Add three bodies for each six inches in height above a standard ceiling.

COLD IS A STATE OF MIND

• Cold is an idea invented by clothing manufacturers.

• Just watch a professional football game in winter and you'll see bare-chested fans flexing their muscles and gamboling gaily during blizzards.

• When mystics go into deep trances and travel to places like Antarctica they never pack long underwear.

THINGS TO DO

• Turn down your heat one degree a week.

• In a year the temperature in your house will be a comfortable 20 degrees and you will no longer need a refrigerator.

• Join a local chapter of the Polar Bear Club.

• The coldest lake or ocean water will feel warm in comparison to the temperature inside your house.

• If you "wimp" out, smear elephant seal grease over your body and you'll be able to go naked no matter how cold it gets.

• **Elephant Seal Grease Benefit**. Because of the powerful smell of the grease, you'll be able to ride the New York subway without being mugged.

5. BAG THE EARTH

*Who are you trying to fool when you drink something
wrapped in a brown paper bag? Next time, try plastic.*

BACKGROUND. The number one problem facing
man today is how to carry things from one place to
another. Up until now, the bag was the solution. But
as soon as we cut down the last tree, the paper bag will go
the way of the dodo, and as soon as we pump the last barrel
of oil, the plastic bag will become as extinct as a solvent
savings and loan.

MARSUPIAL MAN
• The solution is as obvious as it is kinky. Men must be
crossbred with kangaroos so that their beer bellies can be
replaced with utilitarian pouches.
• For women, this "bio-bag" would foil purse snatchers.
• It can be used to keep hamburgers and french fries warm
and soggy.
• The built-in pouch would allow people to discard unsightly fanny packs.

"IT'S IN THE POUCH"
• Expressions featuring the word "bag" would be changed
accordingly.
• In baseball, the home run would become known as the
"four poucher."
• James Brown would sing, "Papa's got a brand new
pouch."

MAGNET MAN
• Another solution is that people and products could be
magnetized.

• As you walked down grocery aisles, items would shoot off the shelves and attach to your body.

• Bigger people, who obviously need more groceries, would have more surface area to hold the products.

• Smaller people would be forbidden from going into grocery stores because heavy items might injure them.

THINGS TO DO

• When you go shopping, only buy one thing at a time.

• Make several hundred trips to the supermarket each week so you'll be able to take advantage of every special.

• If none of these ideas work, learn to consume products on the spot and you'll never have to carry anything anywhere.

6. SAVE JUNK MAIL AND MILLIONS WILL LIVE

Without junk mail you would never know if you won the Publisher's Clearinghouse Sweepstakes.

BACKGROUND. Sure, junk mail is the leading cause of PSS (pouch shoulder syndrome) in mail carriers. And yes, it does waste paper that could be put to better use printing junk bonds. But if junk mail were stopped, millions of lonely Americans would receive no mail at all.

DIDN'T YOU KNOW?
• One person's junk mail is another person's only link with the outside world.

• Psychiatrists predict that the empty mailboxes of America could lead to a rash of suicides.

SIMPLEMINDED THINGS TO DO
• Make sure everyone in your household is on as many mailing lists as possible.

• You'll increase junk mail and help save lives.

• Sell the names and addresses of all your friends to companies that market mailing lists.

• If you have no friends, sell them random names and addresses from the phone book.

• If you have no phone book, give them your own name and address and buy a bigger mailbox.

7. LIGHT UP WITH A THOUSAND POINTS

Every three million years Americans buy enough light bulbs to cover the land surface of the earth. How to attach them to sheer cliffs and steep mountain slopes remains a problem.

BACKGROUND. Ever since Thomas Edison and Joseph Swan invented the incandescent bulb in 1879, Americans have had an ongoing love affair with light. It was in Edison's laboratory that popular phrases such as "a thousand points of light" were born.

INCANDESCENT ADVANTAGE
• Even though fluorescent lamps produce several times more light than incandescent bulbs, they only create one fourth as much heat.

• With "a thousand points of light" (incandescent, of course) in your house you will be able to throw away your furnace.

• In order to cool your home all you'll have to do is turn out the lights.

• Incandescent lights utilize energy at a faster rate, helping to drain the world's supply of oil.

• When all the oil is gone, we can switch to clean nuclear energy and cheap coal power.

• Then we can kiss OPEC goodbye, raise the price of uranium and recover all our money from the foreign countries that have caused us so much grief.

FLUORESCENT DISADVANTAGE
• Little known fact. Fluorescent lamps were developed by the hat industry as electronic balding devices.

• Hat makers, befuddled by exposure to mercury, were convinced that bald men would buy more hats.

• Of course, they had no way to anticipate Yul Brenner or his strange accent.

HOW TO BEAT THE HIGH COST OF LIGHT

• Go to bed when it gets dark.

• If you have to stay up after dark, take your paperback novel or portable TV to an all-night market.

• Work nights and let your employer pay for lighting.

• Live above the Arctic Circle and enjoy 24-hour daylight every summer, then drive down to Antarctica for the winter.

8. CLEAN UP WITH ALGAE RANCHING

You've probably always wondered why marine iguanas never have heart attacks. Obviously, it's their low-cholesterol algae diet.

BACKGROUND. Believe it or not, phosphates from your laundry detergent can grow enough algae to last a lifetime. This algae can lead either to the death of lakes and streams or to your financial fortune. The choice is yours.

ALGAE BOOM
• As trendy California chefs know, algae has less cholesterol than pork, more protein than beer and more flavor than tofu.

• Microwaving algae doesn't affect its okra-like texture.

• Begin algae ranching with your next load of laundry. Make sure your detergent contains plenty of phosphates.

• Divert the waste water into a nearby stream or lake and wait for the algae to "bloom."

• Your sewer line may already be hooked up to a nearby stream, putting you a step ahead of your competitors whose phosphates may be lost at sea.

ALGAE SERVING SUGGESTIONS
• Feature the unique pond-like flavor of algae by serving it with soups, salads and milk shakes.

• Kids will go crazy for algae when you tell them it's pond scum.

• **Algae Alert**. Don't try to grow algae in your swimming pool until you stop using chlorine.

9. DON'T SMOG
YOUR WATER

"I never drink water. Fish piss in it."
—W. C. Fields

BACKGROUND. Crafty developers are asking us to save water with low-flow shower heads that add air to the spray. But do you know what's in the air these days? Picture Los Angeles. (Then again, why bother.)

WATER DANGER
• If too many people save too much water too fast the results could be catastrophic.

• Rivers and dams will all overflow, endangering billions of dollars worth of waterfront property.

• Every dam in the U.S. would have to be torn down to let the extra water flow back to the oceans.

• Officials at the Army Corps of Engineers would suffer a profound identity crisis when ordered to destroy a century's worth of work.

WATER ANTICS
• In Southern California, people water their driveways in the belief that they can grow a new car.

• Vegetarians drink water without realizing each drop contains zillions of tiny creatures.

• Los Angeles residents recently began conserving water in response to a drought.

• The water district then asked for a rate hike to make up for lost revenues.

• Angelenos responded by using more water to keep the rates down.

10. LET'S GET CHEMICAL

Warning: Never let the Surgeon General operate on you.

BACKGROUND. Thanks to the miracles of agricultural chemicals, today we can swallow things we can't even pronounce. Better yet, these chemicals are provided free. What's more, we don't have to waste time deciding which chemicals to eat.

WHY IT'S BETTER NOT TO KNOW
• We sell banned pesticides overseas that come back to us on crops from other countries.

• This benefits both the foreign country and the U.S. consumer who gets it in the end.

• Plastic food wrap is loaded with "plasticizers" that wind up on your food.

• Once these chemicals fully coat your insides, you'll have a Teflon stomach and will be able to eat anything you can fit into your mouth.

THINGS TO DO (OR ELSE)
• Send a hefty check to the chemical company of your choice. Help them stop government regulation.

• Support Jesse Helms in his fight to save tobacco subsidies. Cigarettes are a great way to get chemicals into your body.

• **Toxic Chemical Alert.** If a chemical makes you feel good, don't take chances—just say no.

11. GET INTO HOT WATER

According to anthropologists, fire was discovered when the first caveman needed a hot bath.

BACKGROUND. Humans use hot water. Apes don't. It's critical that hot water be available 24 hours a day. We might wake up one night with the uncontrollable urge to wash the car or bathe the cat.

HOT WATER FACTS
• Most people like to get into it.

• It boils quicker than cold water in case someone is having a baby.

• Without it hot tubs would lose their sex appeal.

• Coffee brewed in cold water tastes like mud.

• Hot water heaters consume 20 percent of the energy used in homes. Obviously that is not enough when you consider that 50 percent of our oil is imported.

HOT IDEAS
• Create your own hot water by running your pipes down into the molten core of the earth

• You'll never have to wrap your hot water heater in a blanket again.

• In fact, by equipping it with a periscope you can convert your hot water heater into a mini-submarine and begin building your own 600-ship navy.

12. PHONE
THE PRESIDENT

1-900-2-IN-THE-BUSH.

BACKGROUND. When George Bush learned that his name refers not only to minor league baseball but also to plant life, he declared himself the environmental president. He also came out in favor of drilling for oil in the Alaskan wilderness when he discovered it was "bush country."

BUSH BUSY SIGNAL
• Be patient; the president's phone is usually busy. Reading lips over the telephone is difficult and time consuming.

• When you finally get him on the phone, tell him you support his decision to save the economy before saving the environment. After all, what good is an environment without an economy to exploit it?

• Tell him you support his plan to replace the ozone layer with a Star Wars shield.

CALL THE PENTAGON
• Tell them the environmental damage created by U.S. military bases around the world is okay. After all, protecting the peace of the world is more important than protecting a piece of the world.

CALL THE EPA
• Don't be surprised if they're all out to lunch.

CHECK YOUR PHONE BOOK
• If it didn't require three or more trees to make it, the town you're living in is too small.

13. PAINT THE TOWN (CADMIUM) RED

Is paint toxic? Why do you think all those Neolithic painted caves are filled with human bones?

BACKGROUND. The miracle of paint is that it can be used to decorate and brighten the world and at the same time to degrade the environment.

PAINT THE EARTH
• If everyone in the world went through paint at the same rate as Americans, 20 billion gallons could be used each year. Is that too much to hope for?
• That's enough to paint the moon but not the earth. Nice try.

IF IT AIN'T HEAVY METAL, PAINT IT AIN'T
• If paint wasn't made with toxic heavy metals such as cadmium, artists would live too long and paint too many paintings.
• Museums would become as overcrowded as jails.
• The average price of a painting would dip precipitously.
• Without the bright colors of heavy metal paints, Japanese connoisseurs would stop attending art auctions and go back to buying up the U.S.

SUPPORT YOUR LOCAL ARTIST
• Join the Committee to Put Heavier Metals into Paint.
• Paint your wagon as often as you can.
• Write the NEA and urge them to only fund artists who use toxic paint for wholesome purposes.

14. GAS PUMP—HOME APPLIANCE OF THE FUTURE

"Regular or Ethyl?"
—Fred Mertz, *I Love Lucy*

BACKGROUND. Automobiles are reproducing faster than people. As more and more cars hit the road, the chances of finding gas are decreasing. If another energy crisis occurs your car will be as worthless as an office building in Houston.

BECOME YOUR OWN OIL COMPANY
• Convert your abandoned fallout shelter into an underground gas station and buy gas directly from your local refinery.

• You'll be able to issue your own credit card to yourself.

• You'll make extra money charging yourself for air and those nifty blue paper towels used to clean windshields.

• When you ask yourself for directions, you can laugh hysterically and claim you don't even know which county you're living in. Then you can sell yourself a fifty-cent map for five dollars.

DON'T LET THE BUCK STOP THERE
• Once you start pulling in the big bucks with your own gas station, buy your own refinery.

• You'll be ready to compete with the big boys and amass your own single-hulled tanker fleet.

EXPLORE FOR YOUR OWN OIL
• Once your infrastructure is in place, you will want to get into the most exciting area of the oil industry—oil exploration! Just give Neil Bush a call and you'll be home free.

15. THERE'S NO ZONE LIKE OZONE

The first report of holes in the atmosphere came from Commander Cody and the Lost Planet Airmen, a rock-and-roll band that has been lost in the ozone since the '60s.

BACKGROUND. Contrary to popular opinion, holes in the ozone layer are not a threat to mankind. In fact, they are a useful evolutionary tool that will stimulate us to become nocturnal. Once Americans begin working and playing at night, we'll no longer have to worry about the burning ultraviolet rays of the sun. Our new national motto will be, "The nighttime is the right time." And we'll finally rid ourselves of that summertime absurdity—daylight saving.

HOLEY NECESSITY
• Without holes in the ozone, the space shuttle would never get into orbit.
• Holes in the ozone are also flyways for UFOs out on galactic joyrides.
• They permit pollution to leak into outer space, informing other planets that there is no intelligent life on earth.

OZONE SHIELD CAUSES SMOG
• Some scientists claim that smog is actually caused by the ozone layer.
• They insist that smog is the best protection we have against ultraviolet radiation.
• These scientists are requesting 100 billion dollars from the government to test their theory by covering the earth with smog.
• After all, what good is an ozone shield that can't even stand up to deodorant spray?

SMOG-CONDITIONING
• Cars are the answer to the ozone problem!

• Ever conscious of the cosmic balance, Detroit is building cars with engines that create ozone-producing smog and air-conditioners that leak ozone-destroying gases.

• **Air-conditioner Alert**. Since smog has replaced air in most major cities, air-conditioners are becoming obsolete and cars will soon be equipped with "smog-conditioners."

• Without smog-conditioners cars couldn't be driven and the cosmic balance would be lost.

• Trees would once again outnumber parking lots, resulting in too much oxygen and not enough metered spaces.

THINGS TO DO
• Never go outside.

• Wear aluminum foil clothes to reflect the sun.

16. CREATE A BATTERY BONANZA

If potatoes can power a clock, can batteries be scalloped?

BACKGROUND. Batteries bring good things to life. Battery-powered stuffed animals give children an opportunity to observe extinct and endangered animals in the privacy of their own home. They are the perfect pets for apartment and condo dwellers. You can remove their batteries if they get too noisy or begin leaking heavy metals on the rug. And, you don't have to housebreak them.

BATTERIES ARE FUNNIER THAN LIFE
• Tests administered at major universities prove that unless toys are battery-powered, children will ignore them, and rightly so.
• Tests administered at junior colleges reveal that if adult toys are not battery-powered, adults won't play with them, even in the privacy of their own bedroom with another consenting adult.

BOOMING BOXES
• The most important use of the battery, next to supplying the juice for the portable electric-powered nostril-hair clipper, is to power the boom box.
• Many historians claim that the Japanese invented the boom box as revenge against us for making them retain their Emperor after they lost World War II.
• The real story is that the Japanese gave us the boom box in return for teaching them how to build cars.

THINGS TO DO

• Join the National Boom Box Association and work to oppose all laws requiring the registration of hand-held boom boxes.

• Support the International Stuffed Animal League's campaign to replace all African wild animals with battery-powered scale models and end unsightly interspecies carnage.

• Help the timber industry's efforts to transistorize the endangered Spotted Owl.

• Ask your local hardware store to start stocking nuclear-powered batteries.

17. JOIN THE CHEMISTRY SET

Take a toxic holiday, stay at home.

BACKGROUND. Thanks to the efforts of the chemical industry, the American home has become a "toxic paradise." In fact, there are so many toxic substances in a typical household that if the EPA ever got around to doing its job, most homes would be classified as Class-A hazardous waste dumps.

PROFIT FROM TOXICS
• Your familiarity with toxic products such as drain cleaner and moth balls may qualify you for a high-paying job in the chemical industry.

• You can turn your house into a hazardous waste dump and make a fortune disposing of your neighbor's toxic waste.

• Once your house is filled with toxic products, apply to the EPA superfund for millions of dollars to clean up your dump.

• **Superfund Payout Alert.** Don't expect the money in your lifetime.

BITE THE BULLET
• Living in a toxic-free environment could cause severe withdrawal pains.

• As the tobacco industry has proved, people and chemicals have a strange attraction for one another.

• If you can learn to live with toxic chemicals, you will gain a competitive edge over more robust species (such as cockroaches and earwigs.)

18. BUY MORE APPLIANCES

The first electric appliance was Benjamin Franklin's lightning-powered kite. Unfortunately, it proved a total failure with the public because it could only be flown during severe thunderstorms.

BACKGROUND. Anthropologists call man the appliance-using animal. When other vertebrates are offered the chance to use appliances, they either ignore them or attempt to eat them. For example, when one million monkeys were given one million word processors, not one of them wrote *Hamlet*. (However, several did get jobs writing for network TV and have been nominated for Emmys.)

APPLIANCE REQUIREMENTS
Unless you own over 100 appliances, including those listed below, you are considered appliance deficient by the Institute of Applied Appliances:

Electric Vegetable Scrubber

Wah-wah Peddle

Electric Egg Scrambler

Shaving Cream Heater

Electric Nose Clipper

Electric Wok

Electric Pepper Grinder

Bikini Waxer

Electric Potato Peeler

Electric Toenail Clipper

• **Appliance Alert.** Use energy efficient appliances. The more energy you save, the more you'll have when new appliances become available.

• You know you have enough appliances when you throw the switch on your frozen-waffle toaster and the entire state blacks out.

THE ULTIMATE HOME APPLIANCE

• The Home Nuclear Reactor (HNR) will free you from the tyranny of OPEC and your local utility company.

• The Home Nuclear Reactor is small enough to fit into your abandoned fallout shelter yet powerful enough to run an infinite number of home appliances.

• Free with every Home Nuclear Reactor sold will be emergency instructions in case of mini-meltdowns.

• Also included are free directions on how to assemble your own home-size atom bomb from your own nuclear wastes, enabling every owner of the HNR to become a dominant military power in his own neighborhood.

19. LIVE FOREVER WITH STYROFOAM

If the Venus de Milo had been made of Styrofoam, she would still have arms.

BACKGROUND. Ever since man was cursed with mortality in the Garden of Eden, he has struggled to leave his mark on earth. When he realized that stone and even metals don't last forever, he experienced a profound existential crisis. But then in 1937, Dow Chemical invented Styrofoam, and man had discovered a material that would not only help eat the ozone but would survive Armageddon.

COOLER MAN
• Millions of abandoned Styrofoam coolers will be discovered by archaeologists of the future, and 20th-century *Homo sapiens* will be known as "Cooler Man," *homo picnicien.*

• The Styrofoam cooler will be symbolic of Cooler Man's desire to be close to the earth by having a picnic.

• Exactly what went into Cooler Man's cooler will be the subject of speculation for thousands of years.

CUP MAN
• Other more sophisticated archaeologists will classify us as "Cup Man," *homo cupien.*

• They will maintain that the Styrofoam cup speaks volumes about the size of our lips.

FOREVER PEANUTS
• Styrofoam peanuts were originally invented as practical jokes for elephants, monkeys and baseball fans.

20. DROP IT IN THE OCEAN

The highest mountains and the deepest valleys are cleverly hidden under the oceans of the world.

BACKGROUND. If oceans weren't available for dumping, then in no time at all civilization would disappear under its own garbage.

DEMONS OF THE DEEP
• Ancient myths tell of demons lurking in the ocean waiting to devour anyone foolhardy enough to go surfing.
• The practice of ocean dumping was an early attempt to placate these demons with leftovers.
• Modern man continues this practice by cleverly substituting toxic waste.
• **Ocean Dumping Alert.** As more garbage is dumped into the oceans, the sea level is beginning to rise, threatening coastal cities and Club Med resorts.

BEACH FIX
• Thanks to the medical industry's use of the ocean as a medical waste dump, a new marine organism has evolved called the syringe fish, *Ichthycus syringus*.

THINGS TO DO
• Fill your bathtub with salt water, garbage and toxic waste to simulate your local beach.
• If your bathtub is deep enough the Navy may even contribute a couple of obsolete nuclear submarines.

21. BRING BACK THE DINOSAURS

The more we learn about the extinction of other animals, the easier it will be for us when it's our turn to go.

BACKGROUND. About 60 million years ago dinosaurs suddenly vanished, leaving only fossil bones behind. Was this the result of natural events, or did we get rid of them because we needed the oil? What we do know is that if early man had developed a taste for dinoburgers, brontosauruses would be grazing in the feedlots of America today.

METEOR MADNESS
• One theory claims that a giant meteor hit the earth with such force that it caused the earth to vibrate for ten thousand years.

• This unprecedented vibration was so intense that it shook the teeth out of every dinosaur, and they starved to death.

TOO BIG FOR THEIR BRITCHES
• Bible experts say that dinosaurs were kicked off the ark because they kept stepping on the other animals.

• Scientists claim they got so big that their legs were no longer able to support them.

• And when they fell over they hit their heads on the ever-present rocks of the Stone Age and died.

• This theory is plausible, because everyone knows that dinosaurs refused to wear crash helmets.

THE SIMPLE TRUTH
• In the Mesozoic era, dinosaurs were unable to hatch their eggs because the White House misappropriated them for the annual Easter egg hunt.

• Japanese collected the eggs because next to whales their favorite food was dinosaur egg sushi.

THINGS TO DO
• Retrieve dinosaur eggs from natural history museums and incubate them in your microwave. You could be the one who brings these gentle beasts back from oblivion.

22. COLLAR YOUR RAT

Christo, the zany conceptual artist, is planning to encircle the earth with flea collars for a project he calls "Dog Earth."

BACKGROUND. Every year Americans spend more money on flea collars for cats and dogs than was made by the movie *Die Hard II*. These collars contain powerful pesticides, so it's silly to use them to kill dog and cat fleas when fleas that live on the brown rat can transmit the bubonic plague. Obviously, we're putting flea collars on the wrong animals.

RAT FACTS
• With the proper lighting and several Barry Manilow albums, one rat couple can produce over 350 million offspring in just three years (provided they ignore biblical incest laws).

• When a rat looks up into the night sky and sees a bat, it has living proof that angels exist.

RAT COLLARS
• Flea collars for rats are a growth industry.

• Neighborhoods have thousands more rats than dogs or even cats.

• Rats are incredibly vain and are dying to wear anything that's the least bit trendy.

• Rats are notorious wannabes. If you can get one rat to wear a flea collar, every other rat in the neighborhood will be wearing one in less than an hour.

THINGS TO DO
• As a sign of rat solidarity, lobby Congress to ban the use of rats for experimental purposes.

• Write President Bush and urge him to meet with rat leaders. There's a good chance he already knows some.

23. FLUSH
FOR POWER

The flush toilet was invented in New York to keep alligators that live in the sewers from getting into people's bathrooms.

BACKGROUND. Every time a toilet is flushed, potential hydroelectric energy is lost down the drain. If this plentiful and cheap energy could be utilized, it would daily exceed the energy equivalent of all the oil spilled by the *Exxon Valdez*.

THE FLUSHING MEADOWS PROJECT
• Scientists working at a secret laboratory in Flushing Meadows, New York have developed a promising weapon in the war against diminishing energy supplies—the Power Flusher.

FLUSH POWER
• The fruit of the Flushing Meadows Project is the state-of-the-art Power Flusher that can be installed in any white ceramic toilet.
• Every flush generates six watts of pure electrical energy.
• Electrical zip cords can be run from the toilet to all the appliances in your home.
• When connected to your TV, the Power Flusher requires three flushes for a 30-minute sitcom, provided you don't watch the commercials.

MORE WATER THAN OIL
• Some television critics complain that using the Power Flusher to view *Lifestyles of the Rich and Famous* is a waste of energy.
• But don't forget, water is a renewable resource.

• We will run out of oil, coal and uranium, but it will always be raining on someone's parade.

• In case of water shortages, people can limit their television viewing to typhoons and floods.

• **Flushing Alert.** Before flushing make sure the Tidy Bowl man has come ashore.

24. TAKE SHOWERLESS SHOWERS

*The first showers were taken by naked people who got caught
in thunderstorms while carrying bars of soap.*

BACKGROUND. While no one can deny the
therapeutic benefits of a three-hour hot shower,
alternatives should be offered to people who refuse
to get naked or get wet.

SHOWER CAP AND GOWN
• Fear of nakedness usually stems from corpophobia (fear
of your own body), but efforts to create shower suits and
dresses to complement shower caps have invariably failed.

• Clothes to cover the body's nakedness only remind the
neurotic that he does indeed have a body.

• No matter how many layers of clothes are put on, the
naked body is still in there trying to get out and expose itself.

SHOWER SOLUTIONS
• Believe it or not, sandblasting was invented as a shower
alternative by Saharan tribesmen who had no water but lots
of sand.

• After surviving blinding sandstorms they felt clean and
refreshed.

• Cynics suggest this was actually because after taking
shelter under a camel, even a mud bath would make you
feel clean.

• **Sandblast Alert.** Cement company executives are quick to
point out that sand is not a limitless resource. Using it for
three-hour sand showers would soon deplete world sand

supplies, closing beaches, putting the lid on playground sandboxes and ultimately threatening the completion of the paving of the earth.

DUST LUST

• Dust Bowl Industries markets the Santa Fe Trail Dust Shower and reminds us that even though dust is not a renewable resource it can be found everywhere in the universe.

• People who swear by the Dust Shower are thrilled that they don't have to powder themselves after showering.

25. JUST SAY YES TO OIL

*Every 32 years the U.S. dumps enough oil into the sea
to cover every ocean on the face of the earth. Obviously,
we are going to need to discover more oceans to maintain
our way of life.*

BACKGROUND. Oil is proof positive that not all addictive substances are necessarily bad. It has enabled us to create such wonders as the 24-hour mini-mart, the drive-in church and that great American sport—cruising the strip.

OIL IS GOOD JUNK
• Oil is the most addictive substance the world has ever known.
• Let's face it, lots of people quit smoking but only the dead stop using oil.
• Gasoline is the main source of speed for most Americans.
• It makes America what it is today.

OIL PUSHERS
• Although gasoline is not sold in schoolyards, it is available on practically every street corner in America.
• Some stations are even open 24-hours a day so you can get gassed in the middle of the night and play chicken with the ghost of James Dean.
• Even though they realize how addicted we are, gasoline companies spend millions of dollars on TV advertising just to bring us our favorite shows.
• They do this knowing that while we're watching TV, it's impossible to use their products.
• They even sponsor shows on PBS that only Bill Moyers and his family will see.
• Short on cash? The oil companies will even give you a credit card to keep you buying what you desperately need.

FOREIGN OIL PUSHERS

• Because of a quirk in nature, most of our oil is located in foreign countries.

• These countries actually force us to pay for our own oil.

• The next thing you know, they'll start asking us to send hostages in exchange for our oil.

THINGS TO DO

• Use oil and oil-related products as fast as you can.

• The faster you use oil, the less chance there is to spill it.

• Get immunized against the oil-eating bacteria that are being developed to devour oil spills.

• Once those bacteria finish eating all the oil, they're going to be awfully hungry.

• Make a bumper sticker that reads, "When oil is outlawed, oil will still be on the hands of outlaws."

• And remember, oil is an essential ingredient in asphalt, without which man cannot hope to pave the earth.

26. BECOME ILLITERATE, SAVE A TREE

In 1987, Manhattan school children constructed a life-size model of the Empire State Building using papier mâché made from a single copy of the Sunday New York Times.

BACKGROUND. Every year 27 million trees are transformed into Sunday newspapers. Even though these trees must eventually come down to make way for highways, parking lots and shopping malls, this represents a gross misuse of America's dwindling supply of timber (and shade).

FUEL OF THE PAST, FUEL OF THE FUTURE
• A little known fact is that during World War II, when gasoline was in short supply, people modified their gas engines to run on wood.

• It's imperative that we save our forests so that when we run out of oil we'll still have thousands of square miles of timber to burn.

• You can bet that OPEC leaders will be getting hot under the collar. Between them the OPEC countries have a grand total of 38 trees, only two of them over 25 feet tall.

ILLITERACY CAN SAVE OUR FORESTS
• For years, press critics have recognized that America's forests must be protected from Sunday editions of the newspaper.

• That's why television was invented.

• Television guaranteed to get people's noses out of the Sunday paper and glue them to the screen.

• But actually the public, which now watches 33 hours of television a day, doesn't buy the Sunday paper to read: people buy it so their neighbors won't think they're illiterate.

• When everyone becomes illiterate, we can free ourselves from this silly status symbol.

THINGS TO DO

• Steal newspapers from neighborhood lawns.

• If people don't get their papers for 40 days there is a good chance they'll cancel their subscriptions.

• Start a rumor that newspaper ink contains LSD.

• Now that the Supreme Court has ruled that opinion can be libelous, sue your local newspaper for printing editorials.

27. PACKAGE YOURSELF

Advertising was invented so that people who had nothing to sell could still participate in a market economy.

BACKGROUND. Americans believe that when they buy something they are paying for what's in the package. In truth, they are paying for the package. What's in it is merely there to give the package an appealing shape.

THE PERILS OF PACKAGING
• Many items are so beautifully packaged that it takes an iron will to open them.

• Trudy Flowers of Downer's Grove, Illinois has 5478 boxes of English designer soap that she is unable to use because she refuses to unseal the wrappers.

• Mrs. Flowers is now living in a tent in the backyard because the house is filled to the ceiling with unopened products.

PEOPLE PACKAGING
• The fashion industry packages people so they will appeal to one another.

• Without attractive fashions people would only associate with their pets.

• Fashion packaging enables important cultural events like the Oscars to take place.

PLASTIC PEOPLE PACKAGING
• Through the miracle of plastic surgery people can alter their body package to look like their favorite Hollywood celebrity package.

• Some movie stars use plastic surgery to make themselves look more like themselves.

• Michael Jackson is using facial packaging to go where no pop star has gone before.

28. LIVE IN A GLASS HOUSE

A matched set of highball glasses engraved with the cartouche of Amenhotep I, who reigned from 1545 to 1525 B.C., proves that glass can last thousands of years and that the Egyptians liked to party.

BACKGROUND. If glass has been around since the ancient Egyptians, it has obviously seen better days. If you've ever stepped on a piece of glass in the sand, you know it should be totally banned, except for export to countries without beaches.

GLASS STOPS PROGRESS

• If glass is an outmoded technology are plastic bottles the solution?

• You must be joking. The only advantage to plastic containers is that they can be turned into polyester suits.

• Instead of plastic bottles we need plastic pipes—tubes that link the processing plant to the home.

• You want catsup, you push a button and it's pumped directly into your barbecue area.

• A catsup meter records your purchase and sends you a bill at the end of the month.

• Even pickles and matzo balls will be tubed directly into your kitchen.

• Glass bottles and jars will become collectors' items.

• Their value will skyrocket and they'll disappear from the landscape.

• Japanese collectors will drive the price of Coke bottles so high that only heavily endowed museums will be able to own them.

GLASS HOUSES HOLD NO SECRETS
• The only modern use of glass should be in housing.

• Crime and immoral behavior will disappear from America when everyone is required to live in a glass house.

• The "viewed" life is the moral life.

• In the old days people behaved well because they believed God was watching everything they did.

• But in the 19th century, Nietzsche mistakenly published an obituary for God (it was supposed to be for his pet schnauzer).

• Chaos ensued and the collapse of moral standards led directly to two world wars and the invention of Twinkies.

• When we live in glass houses, TV monitors will record everything we do.

• Taped excepts from our daily life will be seen on *America's Funniest Home Videos* or *America's Most Wanted*.

• America will rid itself of all its bad actors.

THINGS TO DO
• Save enough glass to build your dream house.

• Figure out how many products you buy in bottles and jars and install that many plastic tubes in your kitchen.

• Make sure the tubes reach all the way to the street so the Gatorade people won't have trouble hooking you up.

• Anticipate the future. Develop a line of see-through clothing to complement your see-through house.

• Since all criminals will be caught and punished, confess your crimes in advance and save yourself the trouble of having to actually commit them.

29. FORGET THE RAINFOREST

Every second, two acres of the world's rainforests is converted into usable grazing land and parking lots.

BACKGROUND. Every time a civilization appears the first thing it does is cut down all the forests. Then the civilization disappears. It's the normal life cycle.

ALL FORESTS DISAPPEAR
• One of today's most far-seeing nations, Malaysia, houses its department of forestry headquarters in an ultra-modern building designed to look like a tree stump.

• With the eradication of Pacific Northwest rainforests, the spotted owl is swiftly evolving into a new species, the "seldom-spotted owl."

CAN ROCK CONCERTS SAVE RAINFORESTS?
• No way, Jose.

• Sting couldn't do it.

• Madonna couldn't do it.

• The only pop star who stands a ghost of a chance is Elvis.

• Maybe if he knew that one in four pharmaceuticals come from a plant in a tropical rainforest, he'd jump on the bandwagon and stage a comeback. Think what Las Vegas could charge for his second coming.

• But don't hold your breath.

• On second thought, if you can't breathe carbon dioxide maybe you'd better hold it.

THINGS TO DO
• Support your local lumberjack.

• Once the forests are gone they'll need all the help they can get.

• They may even evolve into a new species called the "never-spotted lumberjack."

EASIER DONE

THAN SAID

30. KEEP THE WORLD SAFE FOR DUMPING

One world's toxic-waste space transporter is simply another world's UFO.

BACKGROUND. At a recent meeting of the Galactic Association of Hazardous Waste Processors, it was agreed to use Earth as a galactic disposal site. When the representative from the planet Benzo suggested that the furless earthlings would protest, the delegate from Dud laughed, "They don't object to their own waste, why should they object to ours."

SPACE WASTE FACTS
• Space waste is as safe as earth waste, it's just a little shinier.

• Several billion barrels of space waste have been found at an underground Air Force storage facility.

• Reports indicate it will soon be marketed nationally under the name "saucer sauce."

• The distributors hope it will replace tartar sauce.

• They recommend it be served with fresh fish containing PCBs and dioxin.

SPACE WASTE ADVANTAGES
• It assures us that there is intelligent life in the universe.

• Space waste proves that we have something in common with extraterrestrials.

• As soon as Star Wars is in place, we can start charging the galactic garbage trucks a landing fee.

SPACE WASTE DISADVANTAGES
• Once earth is filled with space waste, we'll have no room left for our own garbage.
• Even our favorite dump, the third world, will be filled to the brim.
• The third world desperately needs our waste so they can develop their economies and be just like us.

THINGS TO DO
• The Society for the Prevention of Space Dumping advocates coating the earth with teflon. (Naturally, it would first have to be paved.)
• Then when space garbage is dumped on earth it will slide back into space (given proper weather conditions).

31. THERE'S NO PLACE LIKE A PARKING SPACE

In Los Angeles, a recent survey revealed that at any given moment 63% of all cars on the freeways are being driven simply because there are no available parking spaces.

BACKGROUND. Aside from the obvious aesthetic value, one of the main reasons for paving the earth is that once it's paved there will finally be enough parking spaces. Millions of motorists who are now unable to stop their cars will be able to get out of their vehicles, stretch their legs and run like maniacs to the nearest restroom.

STAKING YOUR CLAIM
• A parking space is prime real estate: once you find one, claim it as private property and begin remodeling.

• One rule of thumb in choosing a permanent parking space is to find the worst spot in the best part of town.

• If the spot is occupied, drive around the block until it becomes free.

• **Drive Around The Block Alert.** Before beginning to circle the block, pack enough food to last at least two weeks.

• If the car doesn't leave by the time you run out of food, assume the owner is deceased and call a tow truck.

REMODELING YOUR SPACE
• Now that you've parked you'll want to decorate your parking place.

• Concrete planter boxes are ideal for flowers or a herbaceous border.

• A colorful canvas canopy is not only visually attractive but also protects your valuable paint job.

• A chain-link dog run around the perimeter will give your space that modern hi-tech look and be perfect for your highstrung doberman.

32. PRESERVE PLASTIC FRUIT

In a national supermarket survey, 94 out of 100 Americans chose plastic fruit over the tree-grown variety because plastic fruit has a longer table life and never attracts flies.

BACKGROUND. It's no secret that Americans eat far too much food in a desperate attempt to keep our farmers employed. But as we become more health conscious we are beginning to recognize that the real value of food is its visual beauty. That's why farmers use pesticides to keep fruits looking good enough to eat.

VEGETABLE COSMETICS
• Pesticides are the cosmetics of the agricultural world.

• It's the word "pesticide" that causes all the problems.

• The cosmetic industry wouldn't even exist if its products were called "blemicides."

• Therefore, the solution to the problem of pesticides is to re-name them "vegemetics."

FEAR OF FRUIT
• Fear of fruit is the result of the incident in the Garden of Eden.

• Adam and Eve ate a forbidden fruit, probably a mango.

• Mango is short for "man go out of the garden and don't come back."

• Since then people have equated fruit with sin.

• That's why most fruit in the U.S. is put in cans and drowned in syrup.

THINGS TO DO
• Join the Fake Fruit Preservation League.

• They are waging a campaign to replace fruit trees with plastic trees bearing plastic fruit.

33. DIAPER THE EARTH

Americans discard enough disposable diapers each year to reach to the moon and back seven times. Now we know why no astronaut has landed on the lunar surface since disposable diapers were invented.

BACKGROUND. Ever since Americans discovered that over 18 billion disposable diapers end up in landfills each year, we have patted ourselves on the back for a job well done. While that's enough to travel to the moon seven times, the President wants to reach Mars while Carl Sagan is still alive. The obvious answer is adult designer disposable diapers.

GOODBYE TO TOILETS
• By using a disposable diaper instead of flushing the toilet, adults could save five gallons of water.

• If a million Americans began wearing designer disposable diapers, the U.S. would save 20 billion gallons of water every year.

• **Adult Disposable Diaper Alert.** Albert Whacknoggin, professor of scatology at the Fetish Institute of Geneva (FIG), warns that adults wearing disposable diapers may experience severe trauma when subjected to retoilet training.

ADULT DIAPER BENEFIT
• No longer will you be held captive to inconvenient bodily functions.

• When nature calls, she'll always get your answering machine.

34. CREATE YOUR OWN CAR CONDO

When people who live in cars get stuck in traffic they can turn off the engine, brush their teeth and go to bed.

If you support the paving of the earth but are still squeamish about all those toxic products needed to create it, why not move into a neutral environment until you're good and ready to take your medicine like a man (or a woman, for that matter).

LEAVE HOME BEFORE IT'S TOO LATE
• Move into your car.
• You'll always be ready to drive to work or the bowling alley.
• If it has bucket seats, sell your car and move into the garage.
• Convert your front and back yard into a duplex.
• If your yard is filled with junk, move into your neighbor's yard.
• **Backyard Alert**. If the yard has been sprayed with pesticides, you might as well stay in the house.
• If you live in a condo, move into a nearby park.
• If you have a pool, dock a houseboat in it.

LIVE OUT ON A LIMB
• A tree is a fabulous place to live.
• If it's high enough, you can take a hang glider to work.
• The view adds to the real estate value of your home.
• **Tree House Alert**. If your tree is in a forest, there's a good chance it will be cut down and shipped to Japan.

35. TRASH IS COLLECTIBLE, OPEN A MUSEUM

To an archaeologist, yesterday's garbage is today's artifact. To a garbageman, yesterday's garbage is what you put today's garbage on top of.

BACKGROUND. The U.S. is currently under attack because our Gross National Product is not gross enough. But that criticism fails to consider the value of our garbage. Ever concerned with their personal savings, Americans have been amassing a wealth of garbage in landfills across the country. Taking this into account, the value of our Gross National Product is so gross that its total grossness is too gross to compute.

BUILD MUSEUMS, NOT DUMPS
• Since trash is destined for museums, why not display your own private collection in your garage.
• The government should build underground museums and fill them with garbage.
• With a clever ad campaign, millions of Americans will wait in long lines to buy tickets.
• Foreign tourists will also gladly pay to see these artifacts of a powerful civilization that once ruled the world and left its garbage on the moon.
• Initially, security costs will be minimal since few people are shrewd enough to steal garbage.
• **Stolen Garbage Alert.** As the exhibits get older, the garbage will become more valuable and security costs will escalate.

36. MAKE WILDLIFE USEFUL LIFE

Pit bulls date to 17th century England when bulls kept falling into pits and the British needed a dog that could lock its jaws onto the bulls and drag them out.

BACKGROUND. Most endangered species are disappearing from the world because people have failed to find a use for them. Let's face it. Who wants to stick around if you're not wanted?

UTILITARIAN ANIMAL FACTS
• Originally sheep were used to herd dogs.

• But since there was almost no demand for dog-hair sweaters, the animals changed places.

• Yaks are prized by Tibetans not as pack animals but because they are naturally funny (*yak* is *yuk* in Tibetan).

• In France, restaurants encourage customers to bring their poodles to dinner since someone's got to eat that rich food.

NEW USES FOR OLD SPECIES
• A killer whale in your swimming pool is the perfect lifeguard: anyone it can't save, it can eat.

• The cape water buffalo, which has been known to upend Land Rovers for fun, is the best beast to ride to work since it is not intimidated by anything on the road smaller than a Mack truck.

• A grizzly bear is a wonderful home security system, an excellent garbage disposal, a no-nonsense babysitter and a genuine piece of disappearing Americana.

• Cover your yard with a huge tent and you can adopt a California condor.

• They will keep your yard free of unsightly carcasses and are big enough to intimidate low-flying malathion helicopters.

• Galapagos tortoises make fabulous footstools and are slow enough for children to ride.

• **Endangered Species Adoption Alert**. Cheetahs, which can rid your home of the swiftest vermin, should be adopted only by people with backyards covering several hundred square miles.

THINGS TO DO

• Interview animals and ask them what they're good for.

• Start an animal employment agency and put these n'er-do-wells to work.

• Send animals to trade schools so they can be retrained for work outside show business.

37. ONE MAN'S LEAK IS ANOTHER MAN'S GAIN

When the White House leaks, call the plumbers.

BACKGROUND. Every year, 25 billion gallons of oil is used by American households to heat the air around their houses. This is done so that when they open their front door they won't get blasted by the bitter cold of the atmosphere.

HEAT LEAKS SAVE ENERGY

• Heat leaking from your house wastes energy only because your neighbor's house was built too far away.

• When homes are built close enough to share the same walls then heat will leak from one to the other.

• Billions of gallons of oil will be saved for more important purposes such as swamp-buggy racing and professional tractor pulls.

LAND ADVANTAGE

• If everyone in the world lived four to a family in an attractive split level ranch-style house containing 2500 square feet, then without question everyone would consider themselves better off.

• Amazingly enough, under these circumstances everyone in the world could live in Texas.

• In fact, Texas would be able to accommodate 11 billion people and still have 20,846 square miles left over for rodeo arenas, honky-tonks and barbecue pits.

• **Living In Texas Alert**. Sociologists question the wisdom of creating an all-Texan world population.

• Another losing season by the Dallas Cowboys could cause everyone to move to Oklahoma.

• Electoral politics in Texas would grind to a halt since no one could afford to buy an election.

MOVING TO TEXAS CHECKLIST
• Work on a drawl so that you won't be identified as a Johnny-come-lately.

• Learn to ride a mechanical bull.

• Tie your toes together so that they'll fit inside pointy-toed cowboy boots.

• **Texas Culture Alert:** Never order pie Alamo for dessert.

38. EAT HIGH ON THE FOOD CHAIN

When saying grace, remember: everything that eats in its turn is eaten.

BACKGROUND. Food is political! It's your patriotic duty to eat as high as you can on the food chain. Just look around. It's the meat-eating countries that dominate the world. As the Swami from Miami says, "You are what you eat, so why be a vegetable. Eat someone stronger and more good looking than you are."

DIDN'T YOU KNOW?
• If American meat-eaters switched to a fat-free diet, they would live longer and end up consuming more of the world's dwindling resources.

• If people didn't eat beef every day, cattle would over-populate range land and soon move into towns and cities.

• Witness what's happened in India.

• If the methane generated by cattle was used as an energy source, OPEC would have to pay the U.S. to take its oil.

THINGS TO DO
• Convert cats and dogs to vegetarianism.

• This will save meat and fish byproducts for human consumption.

RESOURCE
• *Cooking Things That Are Hard to Stomach* by Julia Enfant (Scavenger Books, 1990)

39. DON'T DRINK
THE GRAYWATER

"Graywater, I never touch the stuff—people bathe in it."
—W. C. Fields

BACKGROUND. Graywater is simply water that you've already used. Some people advocate storing it and then using it to water your lawn and garden. But first you need a house, a lawn and garden and the money to install a graywater system. In addition, you have to live in a state where such a system is legal. Wouldn't it be much simpler to pave your yard and install a tennis court?

GRAYWATER ADVANTAGES
• You can raise carp in a graywater pond and create a lifetime supply of gefilte fish.

• You can sell graywater to the Navy to pour around their ships to make them invisible.

• You can fill your swimming pool with graywater to discourage friends and neighbors from swimming in it.

GRAYWATER DISADVANTAGES
• Its color.

• Its name.

• And just the thought that somewhere in your house lurks a large tank filled with water you have bathed in.

• Studies show that people with graywater systems take fewer showers and use less soap because they want to keep their graywater as clean as possible.

THINGS TO DO

• If your tap water smells like Zest and has shampoo bubbles in it, your water district may already be using graywater.

• In that case your graywater could turn out to be blackwater.

• If you have concerns that this is happening in your town, you may want to make your own water from scratch.

• Buy a child's chemistry set and combine two parts hydrogen with one part oxygen and add seasoning to taste.

FOR THOSE WHO HAVE BEEN

"COMMITTED"

40. RETREAD THE EARTH, SOFTLY

"To tire or not to retire? That is the question."
—Hamlet

BACKGROUND. When the rest of the world finally accelerates into the automobile age, we'll be discarding five billion tires a year. That should fill the demand for used tires for backyard swings, Mexican sandals, tugboat bumpers and breeding pens for mosquito ranchers, with enough left over to tastefully decorate the countryside.

USED TIRES CAN SAVE THE EARTH
• Recent astronomical evidence gathered by the orbiting Rubble telescope indicates that a rogue planetoid half the size of the moon is approaching the earth at twice the speed of light.

• Because the impact could take place anytime in the next 10,000 years, we need to erect 30,000-foot-high mountains of tires on all the continents and selected islands so that the rogue planetoid will bounce off the earth.

WORK TIRELESSLY
• Organize teams and scour your area for used tires to build your own protective tire mountain. Don't depend on big government to save your neighborhood.

• If you need more tires, remove them from parked cars and autos stopping at red lights. Cars stuck in traffic jams are also fair game.

POST PLANETOID TIRE USE
• Cover your car with tires. If tires can defend the earth from a rogue planetoid, they can surely protect your car from a rogue motorist.

• Wear a tire turban for protection against rogue elephants.

41. DRIVE FOR LIFE

Every day Los Angeles residents drive over 140 million miles, yet none of them actually go anywhere.

BACKGROUND. Biologists recently discovered the "distance gene" in the human chromosome. This is the gene that tells the body how many miles an individual must drive every day. According to scientists, the gene evolved in the human body around the time the wheel was invented.

DRIVING FACTOIDS
• In Killeen, Texas, the Don't-Stop-For-Us Gas Company will fill your car with gas while you're driving.

• As American motorists intermarry with foreigners, the need to drive is occurring even in populations that have never heard of driver's education.

• Mental illness in the U.S. stems from not having enough cars in the country to satisfy the driving urges of all our citizens.

• If everyone drove as far and as often as they wanted, the entire population would be more spread out and a lot more relaxed.

THINGS TO DO WHILE DRIVING
• Attach a knitting needle to the steering wheel and knit beautiful sweaters, using one hand to steer and the other to perl.

• Attach a hot plate to your dashboard and cook gourmet meals while cruising at 55 mph.

• Then you can open the world's first Drive-By Restaurant.

• Install a portable TV next to your rearview mirror and watch *Days of Our Lives* while keeping an eye peeled for the police.

42. TRANSMISSIONS FROM PLANET AUTO

"Thou shalt have no auto gods before me."
Rule 1, The Owner's Manual

BACKGROUND. The following is an excerpt from a sermon by the Reverend Lee Ima Cocatoo: "Glory hallelujah!! The Kingdom of the Car has arrived! Don't despair that the world is no longer fit for man or beast. Rejoice that it is now heaven on earth for the Automobile, that grandest creation by the grandest of Creators, the great Ford in the sky. So remember, my children, we live only to serve, whether it be self-service or full service."

AUTO-SUGGESTIONS
• If you're still a nonbeliever and don't think cars have special powers, consider this: their roads are everywhere, their fumes fill the air we breathe and they enable teenagers to play hooky.
• Most religions only ask a tithe of ten percent, but the Cult of the Car requires huge amounts of money, and a 500 dollar deductible besides.

RE-IN-CAR-NATION
• Since automobiles allow themselves to be recycled so that they can be "reborn" as new cars, they are the first beings to offer proof of re-in-car-nation.

TRAFFIC JAMBOREE
• Automobiles are highly social beings and require constant interaction with their own kind.
• What we call traffic jams are actually Auto-Jamborees—joyous gatherings of cars.

• These events result in an outpouring of emotion. It's not unusual for cars to honk at each other, squeal their tires, bump into one another or even be so overcome with emotion they have to be towed away from the event.

AUTO-THEOLOGY
• Auto-theologians claim that the "canals" of Mars are actually Martian highways.

• Some believe that automobiles are extraterrestrials. Consider their names—Mercury, Comet, Galaxy, Edsel.

• Heretical auto-theologians assert that highways and city streets seen from outer space are coded messages for car planets in other star systems.

43. BAN THE COMPOST BOMB

A California man was recently cited for improperly storing hazardous waste when his 30-foot-high compost heap caught on fire from the heat generated by decomposing bacteria.

BACKGROUND. If the 24 million tons of leaves and grass that are thrown away every year in the U.S. were put into one large compost pile, the resulting explosion would be equal to five thousand times the energy released by Mount St. Helens and would cover the entire country with up to 18 inches of nutrient-rich compost.

YOU CAN'T DRIVE ON COMPOST ROADS
• One of the main dangers of compost is that you can't drive on it.

• As more and more of the earth's vegetable matter is turned into compost there is less and less solid ground.

• In a few short years the entire surface of the earth will become a spongy mass of explosive compost.

COMPOST IS BLOWIN' IN THE WIND
• When the entire earth is turned into compost, the world could easily blow away.

• Astronomers tell us that outer space is filled with cosmic dust.

• We now know that this cosmic dust is all that remains of planets that once practiced mandatory composting.

• For the earth to remain intact it must be completely paved.

THINGS TO DO
• If you can't stop yourself from composting, remember to keep your compost pile at least 50 yards from your house.

• **Compost Alert**: Be careful when composting vegetable matter or you could become an unwitting accomplice to vegetable reincarnation.

• Vegetable reincarnation leads to a universal dislike of vegetables since no one wants to eat the same brussel sprout twice.

44. PROMOTE WILD LIFE, SAVE SIX-PACK RINGS

Ask not for whom the six-pack rings. This crud's for you.

BACKGROUND. Only a country that could land men on the moon could have given the world the plastic six-pack ring—a convenient way to transport a half-dozen thirst-quenching brews. Unfortunately, American consumers, not realizing the dual purpose of these "sex-pack rings" as marital aids, discard them, menacing marine life and wasting valuable plastic, a non-renewable resource if there ever was one.

LIFE BEFORE PLASTIC SIX-PACK RINGS
• A trip to the supermarket usually resulted in a broken leg.

• Shoppers invariably tripped over loose beer cans rolling down the aisles.

• Beer guzzlers had to be math-proficient since they were required to count to six to buy a six-pack.

• Police had no way to handcuff six-handed suspects.

• Marital sex was rarely attempted.

LIFE AFTER PLASTIC SIX-PACK RINGS
• Six-pack buyers are free from math stress.

• Six-handed bandits are being rounded up.

• Sexual bliss has returned to the family kitchen where it belongs.

NEW USES FOR PLASTIC SIX-PACK RINGS
• Out of shelf space? Attach the rings to your kitchen ceiling and use them to store canned goods.

• Make a fashion statement: wear nose rings and necklaces made from six-pack rings.

• Be really daring: make a fabric-free swimsuit out of six-pack rings decorated with flattened bottle caps.

• Light up your sex life by painting six-pack rings day-glo colors and attaching them to your pajamas.

PLASTIC SIX-PACK RING DISCLAIMERS
• The sexual application of six-pack rings cannot be discussed in this book since the author is currently applying for an NEA grant.

• Anyone considering using a six-pack ring as a marital aid should first consult a professional sex therapist.

• **Sex Club Alert.** Do not, repeat, do not attempt any maneuver or position not seen on network television.

• **Marine Life Alert.** Never discard six-pack rings. In order to protect sea life, store them in a safety deposit box and have them buried with you when you pass away. (Never be buried at sea.)

45. INFLATE MORE PIG BLADDERS

In 1907, Ed Fignoodle, an Iowa hog farmer, inflated a pig bladder and discovered the balloon. This then inspired him to invent birthday parties and political conventions.

BACKGROUND. The first practical use of the Fignoodle bladder balloon was as a "paunchie," which was inserted in a man's pants to simulate a big stomach. Back in Ed's day, a man's paunch signified virtue and dignity. Any man without a paunch was considered a ne'er-do-well and a threat to the marital stability of the community. Now that the balloon has been liberated from men's trousers it symbolizes frivolity.

AMAZING BALLOON FACTS
• The *Titanic* was raised from the ocean by filling its hull with 58 billion latex balloons that were then inflated by professional scuba divers.

• A group of midwestern psychologists claim that balloons exhibit human-like characteristics.

• In nine out of ten tests, balloons that were yelled at either exploded or deflated.

• In one out of ten studies, the balloon expanded until it filled the testing room, crushing the researchers to death.

• In the eleventh test, balloons escaped the laboratory and threatened marine animals.

BALLOONS CAN SAVE THE EARTH
• The Space Shuttle was created to take astronauts into space to fix the holes in the ozone.

• But since the Shuttle rarely flies anymore, the only solution is to fill quadrillions of mylar balloons with ozone and launch them into outer space.

• That's how balloons can save sunbathing as a major American sport.

THINGS TO DO
• Never keep balloons in your wallet and expect them to work in an emergency.

• Urge the President to approve the Safe Balloon Act, which bans pediatricians from using balloons to trick children into thinking it's fun to go to the doctor.

• If a balloon comes up to you on the street and asks for a light, say no. It could be contemplating suicide.

46. SUPPORT YOUR LOCAL SPACE GOAT

Pop-top aluminum cans were invented because beer drinkers kept losing their church keys.

BACKGROUND. Every year in the U.S., billions of aluminum cans never make it to recycling centers. What happens to them? One theory offered by the Vice Presidential Commission for Unexplained Phenomena is that they are being devoured by space goats from Mars who search the solar system for tasty aluminum treats.

SPACE GOAT FACTS
• Some reports indicate that space goats are satisfied with aluminum cans.

• Other reports claim they have been sighted at airports nibbling on airplanes, especially DC-10s.

• This could explain why more and more jets are falling apart in midflight.

• Contrary to published reports, space goats are not the most sexually active creatures in outer space.

• Space rabbits have that distinction.

SPACE GOAT DEFENSE
• Defense experts are demanding an end to the recycling of aluminum cans.

• They want to exchange aluminum for space goat technology.

• Critics charge this is another government plot to swap "beer cans for flying saucers."

THINGS TO DO

• Scatter aluminum cans in vacant lots and along lonely country roads.

• Set up hunting blinds near piles of cans and videotape space goat landings.

• If you get a tape of yourself with a space goat, you'll be invited to appear on the Johnny Carson show.

• Don't settle for the David Letterman show.

• He'll ask you to perform stupid space goat tricks.

47. RECYCLE
YOUR LIFE CYCLE

Now that Shirley MacLaine has popularized reincarnation, we have to stay alive as long as possible to reduce the birth rate.

BACKGROUND. The U.S. Supreme Court recently decided that reincarnation is constitutional and that you can be held responsible for crimes committed during previous lifetimes. (This has led to the use of the *déjà vu* defense.)

THE LAW OF INCREASING RETURNS
• When you leave this plane of existence it is terribly disconcerting to the people close to you, especially if you're operating heavy machinery.

• Suddenly, you have no body to hang your clothes on.

• This "naked soul state" is a profound shock to the ego and leads to a complete loss of personality.

• You then literally disintegrate into thousands of microselves who are born again all over the world, some at the same moment, and others years apart.

• Yes, you could even marry yourself! (Except in Iowa.)

• Even more incredible, you could give birth to yourself!

WHAT TO DO WHEN YOU MEET YOURSELF
• Approach these encounters with caution. After all, you are well aware of what you're capable of doing.

• Remember, even though you are convinced that the you you're meeting is you, the you you're meeting is equally sure that you are really him/her.

• In actuality, neither one of you is totally you since the you that you both are is the sum of all your yous.

- To help socially integrate yourself, begin all conversations with the phrase, "Are you me?"

- If the other replies, "Only if you're me, too," you know you're getting your act together.

- After contacting all your yous, rent a stadium and have a party. Make it a potluck so you can experience your wide variety of tastes.

- You will find that at least one of you will have done all the things that you have been killing yourself trying to accomplish.

- So now that you've already done everything you've ever wanted to do, relax, enjoy life and get to know the you you've always dreamed you were.

48. I NEVER PROMISED YOU A ROCK GARDEN

"It was the most beautiful place I've ever been. There wasn't a living thing as far as the eye could see."—Lunar Astronaut

BACKGROUND. Government scientists, working in a top-secret laboratory during World War II to determine the perfect victory garden, came upon an unexpected phenomenon. After three years they discovered that rocks in their gardens were still alive despite the fact they had never been watered.

ROCKY FACTS

• Obviously, the solution to the water shortage is to plant drought-resistant rocks around your astroturf lawn.

• Most earth rocks will survive for years without watering.

• However, some experts contend that earth rocks do require water and will turn to sand if forced to survive on morning dew.

• Moon rocks come from an environment that has never known rain and are the ultimate drought-resistant rock.

• Since moon rocks are alien creatures, they can flourish despite exposure to pesticides, herbicides and fertilizers.

• Not only that, they thrive on temperature extremes and use less gravity to remain attached to the earth.

THINGS TO DO

• Visit the moon for landscaping ideas for your yard.

• Warn the plants that if they use too much water you'll replace them with low maintenance rocks.

• Play Rolling Stone tapes in the garden to keep your rocks content.

49. STAY THE COURSE

It doesn't matter what your score is as long as you make it to the 19th hole.

BACKGROUND. Some pave the earthers are concerned that people reading this book will think that is all they have to do to bring about the paving of the earth. Nothing could be closer to the truth!

In fact, the paving of the earth is an instinctive human response to the environment and is beyond our control. Besides that, we're progressing beautifully!

Still, some of you are desperate to get involved. Many earth pavers are putting on bake sales to raise money to purchase vacant lots that are in danger of devolving back to a primeval state. Others are placing their bodies on the line to stop enemy species from invading our territory. Witness the winter of 1989 when fearless buffalo hunters risked frostbite to prevent Yellowstone Park buffaloes from trespassing onto denatured private property.

The best way to create the illusion of involvement is to start organizations that will attract likeminded people (hopefully with lots of money) to work on bringing about the inevitable. Here's a list of groups that don't need to be established, but could be if you get the urge.

Center for Asphalt Enhancement
Citizens for Better Cement
Earth Island Parking Lot
Freeway Action Network
James Watt League
Shopping Mall Club
Planet Pavers Unlimited
World Urban Fund
People for More Packaging
Citizen's Warehouse for Radioactive Waste
Friends of the Tarmac
Unplanned Parenthood

50. KEEP IT A SECRET

It's a matter of national insecurity.

Now that you've read this book and been filled with the vision of an astounding future, you're probably wondering whether to dedicate the rest of your life to spreading the good news.

By all means, **do not!** This book contains material of a highly technical nature that requires thousands of readings to fully understand and appreciate.

The author and publisher warn prospective pavers not to attempt any of the projects described in the book unless they have first checked with state and federal authorities and their local cement company.

Whatever you do, **do not write** to the author about your ideas for paving the earth. Chances are somebody else already thought of them. The bottom line is that the paving is already happening fast enough, thank you very much!

So friends, fanatics and fatalists, **pave away.**

And remember, dear reader, three rights make a left. May the traffic lights of life always be green for you.

BUT SERIOUSLY, FOLKS

We live in a world where our daily activities are having a profound effect on the earth. It must be continually reaffirmed that now is the time for all of us to do what we can to change our relationship with the planet that sustains us all.

In writing *50 Simple Things You Can Do to PAVE the Earth*, I have tried to use humor to illuminate the major environmental problems we face today—and perhaps shine a bit of comedic light on a lifestyle that is threatening to "naturally select" us off the planet. It has been demonstrated that humor can have a positive impact on disease and it is my fervent hope that it can also help to heal the earth.

Darryl Henriques
Los Angeles, 1990

ABOUT THE AUTHOR

Award-winning stand-up comedian Darryl Henriques is at the forefront in promoting environmental awareness through comedy. He has appeared nationally on public television and HBO and has performed for Greenpeace, the Abalone Alliance and Friends of the Earth. He is known as the "Bob Hope of the California Conservation Corps" for his many appearances at their camps.

As an actor he has appeared in such movies as *The Right Stuff* and *No Way Out* and television shows like *Star Trek: The Next Generation* and *Remington Steele*.